PRAYING
WITH KATII

PRAYING WITH KATIE

God, My Cat, and Me

Don Holt Jr.

Andrews McMeel
Publishing

Kansas City

00 01 02 03 04 QUF 10 9 8 7 6 5 4 3 2 1

Library of Congress Cataloging-in-Publication Data
Holt, Don.
 Praying with Katie : god, my cat, and me / Don Holt, Jr.
   p. cm.
 ISBN 0-7407-1157-1
   1. Christian life. 2. Cats—Religious aspects—Christianity. I. Title.

BV4501.2 .H573 2001
248.3—dc21   00-062074

Book design by Holly Camerlinck

For pilgrims

who hope for wise companions along the way

CONTENTS

ACKNOWLEDGMENTS

I am grateful to:

Tyanne, student assistant at the library of the College of St. Catherine, who brought Katie to

Connie, who brought her home and cared for and shared in her life;

Lutheran Social Services, which fired me and thus inadvertently provided the time to follow Katie's leading;

the labor unions that fought for the unemployment compensation that partially supported me during my unchosen idleness, and all the employers and taxpayers who funded that support.

Without these this book would not have happened.

I am also grateful for the indirect contributions of many others:

My parents and the First Presbyterian Church of Oconto, Wisconsin, who first taught me to pray;

the several Presbyterian congregations and Catholic parishes that paid me to pray throughout my career as a religious professional;

the monastic community of St. Gregory's Abbey in Three Rivers, Michigan, which introduced me to the majestic liturgies of contemplative prayer;

the Catholic Worker Community of St. Joseph's House in Minneapolis, Minnesota, which immersed me in the passionate prayer of Catholic social justice;

Walworth Slenger, my psychoanalyst, who helped me venture down into the dark, rich soil of unconscious faith;

and my several spiritual directors, who walked with me in the valley of the shadow and pointed the way to green pastures and still waters.

The extravagance of the Holy One is extraordinary—all these resources created and combined to produce this slim volume. To that One I am also grateful.

INTRODUCTION

I was unemployed.

It was a time of anger, fear, self-pity, and housework.

It was also a time of considerable spiritual uncertainty. I had been ordained as a Presbyterian minister in 1960. For some twenty years I scrambled through several pastorates, none very successfully, gradually drifting away from my inherited Protestantism. The current on which I was drifting carried me into the Catholic Worker Movement and to the office of a Catholic spiritual director. The former gave me a taste of Christian poverty; the latter set me to work on the Ignatian exercises. The combination made me seriously consider joining the Roman Catholic Church.

Enter Katie.

She came to us from the library of the College of St. Catherine, an orphan kitten hidden by my wife's student assistant in her dorm room. Her meowing was beginning to make obvious the fact that some dorm rules were being broken. In a desperate attempt to find her a home, the student brought her to my wife's office in the library.

Katie decided the office desk chair was suitable for napping.

My wife agreed to keep her "for a few days."

Katie had found herself a permanent home.

When Katie entered my life, I was fifty-seven years old. Without a job. Dependent on my wife and parents. Between religions. And with lots of time on my hands in which to pray and lots of issues to pray about.

Katie entered into my prayer practice just as she entered every other part of our lives.

She became for me a spiritual *provocateur* and guide.

One

. . . .

TEACH US
TO PRAY

$\mathscr{I}$t's hard for me to talk to God.

I tend, therefore, to write letters to God instead. I pray with my pen, scribbling free associations instead of speaking them. With a writing board on my lap, I sit and scrawl whatever ideas and images come to mind. Writing is easier for me than conversing. Sharing with the Holy One via pen and paper is easier than sharing through spoken words.

Most early mornings, then, my praying time was spent sitting on our sofa, writing to God.

That was before Katie joined us.

Katie is our cat.

When she became part of our family she also

became part of my morning prayer. As soon as I
sat down she would join me, leaping onto the
sofa, snuggling into my lap, and in the process of
joining me, leading me into new understandings
of old perspectives on prayer. She became a kind
of companion in contemplation, a nonverbal,
purring colleague and guide.

My first reaction to her intrusion was to push
her off the couch. After all, I was *praying* and she
was disrupting this important activity.

My second reaction, however,

> was to note,
>
> and to admit to myself,
>
> how much
>
> I was enjoying her company.

Perhaps she was a gift

> (if not an angel)
>
> from God
>
> and I should accept her as such

and see what happened.

What happened, as I scribbled, was that Katie chewed on my pen and walked on my paper and thereby prevented my pen-prayer. She also rubbed against my face, nestled against my stomach, purred loudly and decisively, and thereby aroused in me some delightfully warm affection.

Her chewing and walking and rubbing and nestling

    lured me,

      even summoned me,

        to a different kind of prayer.

Instead of looking for the presence of God

    in a string of written ideas,

I found myself reaching for God

    in a series of skin sensations.

My prayer, under Katie's guidance, became

    tactile

      rather than

mental.

Instead of

an opening of my mind to God,

an opening of my skin.

Instead of

a stimulating flash of insights,

an expanding glow of happiness.

51414414144443

(Katie just jumped on the keyboard of the word processor; this has become a joint venture.)

For me this was a very different approach to prayer.

Two

. . . .

L O V E

Katie introduced me to a new dimension of love in prayer.

As I sat meditating, she jumped up on my lap, nuzzled my chin, and laid herself like a corsage across my chest and shoulder, closed her eyes and purred. Soon she slept.

I felt loved. She wanted me. She wanted to be in touch with me, to receive strokes and caresses, to feel my warmth, to rest in comfort and closeness.

I felt honored. This little cat was trusting me.

I felt amused by her presumption. She was, without apology, interrupting my important spiritual work.

I felt corrected. She was suggesting that bodily contact is as important to a relationship as mental exertion.

She set me wondering. Might I not be able to love God in the ways that Katie was loving me?

A desire to be close,
    to be in touch,
      to receive strokes and caresses from the
        Eternal,
      to feel warm and safe and comfortable
        with God?

Was this not exactly what I longed for—the experience of stretching out, so to speak, on the breast of God, purring in contentment, safely supported by the everlasting arms?

Katie was modeling for me a relationship that I had wanted for a long time.

Further, if her presumptuous intrusiveness made me so happy, might not a similar trusting intrusiveness on my part make God happy?

Suppose I simply made clear

my wanting

to be present

and in touch.

Suppose I intruded on God

without asking permission,

just jumped on His/Her lap,

as it were.

Suppose I interrupted God's important work

with my own need

for strokes

and warmth.

Might that make the Eternal happy?

A way to "Bless the Lord, O my soul" (and body)? Certainly Katie's wanting to be with me blessed me. She made me happy.

My wanting

to be with God

might likewise bless God

might likewise make God happy.

Simply wanting

might be pleasing.

So I abandoned my cognitive contemplations, leaned my head back against the sofa, closed my eyes, and imagined myself draped and purring on my Lord's shoulder.

Soon I slept.

Never before had I thought of honoring God by falling asleep during prayer. Katie showed me that peaceful sleep was an expression of trust and thus a kind of praying.

And I believe that God is happy to have me stretched like a corsage across Her/His torso, even though I interrupt the divine schedule for the day.

Three

. . . .

JUDGMENT

$\mathcal{K}$atie's insistent snuggling pronounces a kind of judgment on me—an evaluation of my love for God.

Katie loves me because I provide for her. I serve her milk and cat food. I offer her welcome. I scratch her back. I provide body warmth. Her love for me is eros-love. She enjoys my companionship because I make her feel good. She is *not* a feline altruist.

And that is perfectly all right with me. I do not feel used, abused, or exploited. I thoroughly enjoy her company, including her needs and desires, even though I am well aware of her self-serving motivations. Pursuing her own interests

makes her just as much fun to be with as if she
were trying to serve my interests. (Probably more
fun; a self-sacrificial cat whose goal in life was to
make me happy would be an embarrassment. It is
rather her thoroughgoing self-centeredness that
makes her such a delight.)

    She reminds me that

        my love for God

        like hers for me,

           is eros-love.

        I love God because God provides

           food and light and water,

           meaning and hope,

           work and play,

           relationships and solitude

        an unending list of blessings. . . .

    God, by contrast, offers me agape-love.

        Before Katie,

        I sort of assumed,

without really thinking about it,

that I offered agape-love back to God.

At least I wanted to believe that. I did not want to think of myself as loving God only for what I could get from the relationship.

How crass!

How selfish!

How manipulative!

How magical!

How primitive!

Surely I was a better

(more sophisticated)

Christian

than that!

Under Katie's guidance I realized that such a belief elevates me, or plunges me (depending on whether I imagine God as in the heights of heaven or the depths of being), to the level of deity.

I am believing that I love as God loves!

A trifle arrogant.

A trifle inaccurate.

Sin.

The aspiration of Adam and Eve—to become as God. And I was assuming I had made it.

Katie brings me down (or up) to earth
    from
  assumptions of divinity
    to
  hopes for humanity.

As Katie offers me eros-love,
  and pleases me thereby,
so I can offer eros-love to God
  and thereby please Eternity.

As Katie loves me
  for the strokes and warmth and food and
    safety I provide,
So I love God

for all that God provides.

And that is sufficient.

As I am pleased with Katie, so may God be

pleased with me.

Glory to God in the highest,

and on earth peace among men [and women]

with whom He [She] is well-pleased.

—Luke 2:14, RSV

Four

. . . .

CONTEMPLATION

$\mathcal{O}$ften when my wife and I are sitting on the sofa reading or talking, Katie sits at our feet and gazes up at us. She watches us steadily, without blinking.

Her eyes follow our every move
    but
she shows no desire to understand
    us,
    or our activities,
    or to know us better,
    or to do anything,
    other than just gaze at us.

It is hard to comprehend the emotional, cognitive, and spiritual states of this cat when she just sits and stares. I assume she is interested. But it seems to be a disinterested interest. She watches without passion or pretense. She seems to like to do it but attaches no great importance to it.

For me she becomes a model of contemplation. Simply to sit at God's feet and gaze,

> trying neither to understand
>> nor to influence,
> seeking neither to realize joy
>> nor unload grief,
> simply interested in watching God be God.

Much of my praying is a plea for understanding, a request for help. How different is my contemplation of God from Katie's contemplation of us. She is content just to watch us.

If I were similarly content to simply stare at God

> (at work, at play, at rest):

Watching

> the sun rising and setting

would qualify as contemplation,
contemplation of the Divine Without—
of God at play (or is this God at work?)
Watching
hardhats weld and rivet and pour concrete
would qualify as contemplation,
contemplation of the Divine Without—
of God at work (or is this God's play?)
(Unlike Katie, I am trying to understand
instead of just observing.)
Watching
memories and fantasies
drift along the avenues of my consciousness
would qualify as contemplation,
contemplation of the Divine Within—
of God at play (or is this the Eternal work?)
Watching
my own mind,
emptied of plans, images, and ideas,

would qualify as contemplation,

contemplation of God Within—

God at rest.*

When Katie just sits and watches us I find
her interest vastly satisfying, entertaining, dis-
tracting, pleasing, liberating. She asks nothing of
us except permission to stare. She lays no burden
on us except the burden of being there.

("My yoke is easy and my burden is light,"
Jesus said.)

Does God enjoy being stared at?

Would my unblinking attention

satisfy,

entertain,

distract,

please,

liberate,

God?

If I gaze at

God at work,

God at play,

God at rest,

even though I seek nothing—

neither understanding,

nor provision,

nor capacity to serve,

Do I still please God? Do I add to the Eternal blessedness?

*Perhaps this explains why this kind of watching is so hard for me to do. In me God is seldom at rest. There is so much to do to bring me up to snuff that God must work overtime to get it done.

Five

. . . .

PETITION

$\mathcal{K}$atie often wants something from me.

She wants food. At breakfast time she follows me into the kitchen, checks out the plants in the window, then sits down beside her dish and watches me. She is patient. She neither meows nor rubs against my ankles. She simply waits, confident that at some point meat and milk will be provided.

Then she eats.

She never pauses to return thanks. But she does lick her chops when she has finished.

She makes me wonder about the grace I say before each meal.

Am I,

although more verbal,

as grateful,

as she?

She makes me wonder about the faith I pro-
fess. She waits patiently for food, absolutely confident that I will put some in her dish.

Am I,

although more theological,

as trusting

as she?

She does not pray for her daily cat food. She
waits. I pray but do not wait. I hustle to earn and
buy to put food in my dish.

Katie's patient dependence on me reminds
me of my less-than-patient dependence on Power
beyond my skill and energy that provides my
daily bread.

Although her morning petition is usually one
of quiet waiting, often her requests are less

patient, more urgent and intrusive.

She jumps on our bed at five o'clock A.M. and licks our chins and noses and chews our hair until we awake and realize that it is time to play and pet.

(Jesus told two parables about petitionary prayer, one about a bothersome widow, the other about a persistent friend. The widow kept pestering a hard-hearted judge until he gave her justice, just to get her off his case [Luke 18:1–8]. The friend kept pounding on his neighbor's door until the latter got out of bed and lent him bread [Luke 11:5–8]. Jesus used these two stories to illustrate an attitude toward prayer—persistence that keeps bothering God until one finally gets what one asks for.)

Katie keeps after us early in the morning. We brush her off and she comes back. We push her away and she returns. We hide our heads under the covers and she walks on top of us, purring ferociously.

And do we mind?

We do not. At least, not usually. If we minded we would shut the door and keep her out of our bedroom. We don't do that.

Rather, we enjoy her attentiveness, her presence, her persistence, no matter that it interrupts our sleep. If she enjoys our company that much, losing a little sleep is a small price to pay for her affection.

I wonder if God feels about me the way I feel about Katie? Does God leave the door open at night,

> welcoming the time
>> when I will wake up
>> and want to play?
> Should I keep after Him/Her
>> when I feel pushed away,

when God seems to be hiding from me?
Katie persists in her dawn petitions—and I
like it. I think God may likewise enjoy my
persistence.

Six

SELF-
IMPROVEMENT

$\mathcal{K}$atie never seeks self-improvement. She never petitions us to help her become a better cat.

It probably never enters her cat mind that she needs improvement.

When she stares at us or snuggles against us, when she follows us around, she does so either because she enjoys doing so or because she wants something from us. She does not use our presence as an inspiration to become a better cat.

And that is not because she is a perfectly obedient cat. She does not always do our will. She gives us our dawn licking even though we command her to stop. She often refuses to come when called. She sometimes jumps on the dinner table even though we have clearly instructed her not to. She disobeys our commandments and ignores our will.

She even has a Pharisaic streak in her. She over-obeys one of our commandments. She obeys so well our dictum "Thou shalt urinate and defecate only in the cat box" that, if she is outside and needs to relieve herself, she scratches at the screen door to come *indoors* to use her facilities!

She is not, by religious standards, a righteous cat. Yet, despite her breaking of our rules, we love her.

No, more than that: Because she breaks our rules we love her. Her very disobedience is a part of the perfection of her felinity. She is perfectly catlike, and being catlike includes indifference to our desires. We find her independence delightful (most of the time).

Might not God feel the same way about me?
I have been told that the Lord accepts me the
way I am. Might there not be more than mere
acceptance? What if God *enjoys* me the way I
am? Maybe the Holy One takes a certain wry
pleasure in my indifference to the divine will, a
certain amusement in my attempts to get away
with something.

(I remember a Christmas of my childhood in
which some rule breaking by our cats led to gales of
laughter and happy memories. When we went to
church, my mother left the Christmas turkey thaw-
ing on the kitchen counter. We returned to discover
our two cats, one at each end of the turkey, gnaw-
ing away. That violation of our commandments
brought howls of both laughter and anguish at the
time and still fetches a chuckle whenever the
memory of those "naughty" cats is recalled.)

Does God chuckle at my self-seeking violations

of the rules? I have a hunch that even my rule
breaking may give God pleasure because it is so
much a part of my humanity. God designed me to
break rules. When I do so, I am being perfectly
humanlike and in so being I am a joy to the Eternal.

(Did not God sort of set up Adam and Eve
for disobedience? God tells them that they can
eat all the fruit of the Garden except for the fruit
of one tree—sort of like saying, "Don't stick
beans in your ears." Then God makes available
the serpent [if God didn't create the serpent,
who did?] to tempt them to break the rule. The
Lord God was hoping all along that they would
declare their independence and thus become
humans rather than automatons.)

If God enjoys me being who I am, as we
enjoy Katie being what she is, then praying for
help to be better is a mistake. It is unfeline for
Katie; it is unhuman for me.

42

God is happy with me the way I am.

Why should I try to improve? If God is satisfied, why should I be discontent?

When I think of how much of my prayer has been devoted to begging God for assistance in self-improvement, I am both appalled and amused.

Seven

EUCHARIST

After Katie finishes her lunch she usually takes a nap. She wanders around a bit, looking for a comfortable place in which to ensconce herself. She settles in, spends a few moments grooming her paws and whiskers, and then falls deeply asleep.

She enjoys her sense of full-fed well-being.

This morning as I knelt in church after receiving the bread and wine of the Eucharist I found myself comparing my responses to "being fed" with Katie's.

Far

> from looking for a place to sleep,
> I was thinking about going to work—

the things I needed to do,

the things I wanted to do,

the problems with which I had to cope,

my doubts of being able to measure up,

my hopes of working harder

    and better.

          Far

from simply enjoying the experience of

    being filled,

I was ignoring my fullness

and remembering my emptiness,

concentrating on obligations

    that lay in wait for me

        like carnivorous beasts.

          Far

from reveling in my present well-being

I was anticipating my future distress.

I'm not, however, always like that.

After the "big meals" of the year, the holiday

meals of birthdays, Thanksgivings, and
Christmases, I do not expect myself to go to
work. Then, like Katie, I look for a place to
snooze. After meals of celebration I do act like
Katie. At those special times I relish my fullness
and I relax, enjoy, and digest it.

Katie, however, treats almost every meal the
way I treat holiday meals.

For her,

every bowl of milk and dish of cat food

is an occasion

of celebration.

For me

only the grandest meals

rate such a response.

Katie suggests to me that

when I come to the table—

the table of our Lord

or the table in our kitchen—

Perhaps I, too,

    can set aside the future

    to celebrate the present.

Perhaps I, too,

    can enjoy my fullness

    of spirit

    or of stomach.

Perhaps I, too,

    can let myself catnap

      instead of pressing it to strive

until it's dog-tired.

Eight

EXPLORATIONS
OF NOVELTY

Katie came to live with us in the winter-time. Consequently she became a housecat. During the ice and snow of her first months with us she was seldom outside.

When spring came, however, we introduced her to the lawns and sidewalks of the city out-side. Her response was eagerness: consistent, continual eagerness. She always wanted to go out. Thus, when she heard us going down the stairs to the back door, Katie came dashing, scrambling to get ahead of us in order to squeeze through the smallest opening. She prowled back and forth in front of the door, all urgency to escape to the grass and sunlight outside.

As soon, however, as we opened the door for her, her demeanor changed radically. Hesitation; sniff; a cautious few steps through the opening with still enough of her hindquarters remaining in the doorway to preserve the possibility of retreat. Pause; sniff again; peer; then finally, often assisted by a gentle prod from a foot (because we were getting tired of standing there holding the door open, waiting for her to make up her mind), she would stalk with all deliberate speed out into our yard.

Once outside she wriggled and rolled in the grass and on the sidewalk, purely relishing the sensations available.

Many people I know tend to be spiritual housecats, content to live "indoors," within the comfortable boundaries of the religious world in which they began their lives.

To all of us, however, at some point novelty

presents itself. Spring comes. God is willing to let us out into a new world, a world of new sights and smells and tastes, an unfamiliar environment inhabited by strange cats and spiced with risk.

Katie models a response.

When I hear God's footsteps heading for the
>   door,
>   I could go dashing after,
>   eager to discover
>   what is going on.
When the door is opened,
>   I could push halfway through,
>   sniff,
>   peer,
>   pause. . . .

Novelty (a fresh interpretation of a familiar biblical passage; a new doctrine; a new application of an old doctrine; an unfamiliar worship practice; an abstract picture of Jesus) is poten-

tially delightful—but it is not something to
embrace without checking it out.

A cautious pause does not insult

the God

who opens the door.

(Perhaps if I pause too long the divine foot
will gently propel me farther.)

Once safely outside,

I can relish

the sensations available

in the new environment of the spirit.

Some people, unlike Katie, are not interested.
They may hear the footsteps on the stairs but
have no interest in where those steps are heading. In fact, if pressured to go "outside" they will
resist or run and hide. They are housecats, solely
and entirely. Exploration and experience of a
new world beyond the walls that bound their
present existence is not attractive.

Other people, like Katie, go bounding after the One who's heading toward the outside, afraid they might miss something, eager to sample the unknown. But then, unlike Katie, they do not guard themselves against the dangers that might lurk in the unfamiliar. They dash into the new spiritual environment. Rather than sample it cautiously, rather than pause and sniff and peer, they plunge headlong into the novelty, oblivious to risk.

Katie models a cat-wise balance of curiosity and caution. She eagerly responds to the possibilities inherent in the unfamiliar. But she also tests the unfamiliar with considerable caution before she commits herself to it.

I would do well to emulate her eager self-restraint.

Nine

. . . .

TRINITY

$\mathcal{K}$atie lives with two of us, my wife and me.

We both feed her and pet her and talk to her.

She responds to both of us. Sometimes she seems to prefer one of us, sometimes the other. If we are sitting together on the sofa, most often she settles herself between us.

I suspect she perceives us as two persons but one substance. We provide the same services— food, strokes, warmth—but with different styles. We both love her but in two ways, a masculine and a feminine way. We are to her at once a unity and a duality.

I believe in the Triune God. I look to One Source and I receive in three Styles—Father,

Son, and Holy Spirit.
        Does God love me
            in three ways,
                Masculine,
                Feminine,
                and Neuter?
        Are You
            He?
            She?
            It?
            All?

Ten

. . . .

TRAVEL

As I began reading my morning prayer, Katie leaped on my lap and meowed. She wanted me to give her breakfast.

I am unemployed. I hunger for work.

So, like Katie, I also cry out to God,

for feeding,

specifically,

for a job.

I refused to feed Katie this morning. We were going to take her on a five-hour drive and we did not want her to throw up in our car en route. We did not want her making a mess for us to clean up.

So also, O God,

You refuse to feed me,

    refuse to give me the job for which I yowl.

You, too, are taking me on a trip

    and don't want me to get sick

      on the journey.

I understand.

    But I don't like it.

I trust You will give me what I need

    when we reach our destination.

Katie didn't know that she was going on a journey. Nor did she know where she was going. All she knew was that she was hungry and so she came prowling and yowling to the source of supply.

So also, O God,

    I do not know my destination.

    Sometimes I do not even know I am on

      a trip.

What I do know is that I am hungry

    and my hunger is urgent

and so I prowl and yowl

    to the Source of supply.

Lord God, You refuse to answer my prayer to give me what I want. You know I need a job. You know my want is justified. You know I am only asking for what I really need.

Neverthless, You refuse to provide what I ask for. Are You taking me on a trip? If You feed me now, You know I am likely to get sick, I'm likely to throw up, I'm likely to be miserable, I'm likely to make a mess that You will have to clean up later.

So You delay feeding me until we reach our destination. You put off answering my prayer until we arrive at whatever place You are taking me.

Meanwhile, You ask me to endure the trip and trust that the outcome will be worth the comfort.

Eleven

. . . .

IDOLATRY

$\mathcal{W}$e are moving. A stressful time.

As I carried armloads of boxes out the back door, Katie came galloping down the stairs. Apparently she wanted to go out.

So I set one armload of boxes down and held the screen door open for her. "You want to go out, Katie?" I crooned.

She hesitated—then turned toward the boxes, sniffed, and climbed inside one to investigate.

I laughed.

Now I think I would not have laughed had it been my daughter who had done that. Irritated by the interruption, I would have been impatient, demanding. "Come on, kid, let's go. If you want to go out, go out. Make up your mind." I would not have enjoyed standing there, straining to hold boxes with one arm and a door with the other. I would not have been amused by a child who was prolonging my stress.

Why was it so much easier for me to forgive a cat her procrastination than a child?

It is so natural for a cat to sniff and investigate that it is easy to enjoy her doing it—even when it inconveniences me when she does so.

But it is also natural for a child to explore and investigate. Why do I not enjoy that?

I think because I expect my child, but not the cat, to be considerate of me. I assume my child believes that I am deserving of consideration. I assume the cat does not. My child knows that I am "Daddy" and therefore am entitled to be obeyed instantly. The cat does not know that I am a semi-deity; she is not aware of my entitlements.

Therefore I am easy with the cat and enjoy her and I am hard on my child and am angry with her. And it is all because of my self-deification—what some authorities call "sin."

If I did not think of myself as godlike, I would not expect anyone—cat, daughter, wife, boss—to be considerate of me. If I did not believe I was entitled, I would not be offended when cat, daughter, wife, or boss neglected to give me my just deserts. If I did not believe, just beneath the surface of my consciousness, that I was godlike, I would be free to enjoy everyone, cat or person, considerate or not.

Katie's inconsiderateness reveals my self-deification.

Twelve

. . . .

THE CENTER

When it is time to go to sleep Katie precedes us to the bedroom and leaps onto the middle of the bed. She wants to be the center of our sleeping, indeed, the center of our lives.

I've heard it said that God is, or should be, the center of my life. Without thinking very much about it, I imagined God sort of setting Godself down someplace and me arranging and rearranging myself and my life around Her/Him. I sort of assumed that I made the Eternal One the center; God was "there" and I surrounded the Deity with my life.

Katie's bedtime behavior suggests a different image.

She doesn't sit in the middle of the living room and wait for us to arrange ourselves around her. Not at all. Instead she figures out where we are going, dashes ahead of us, and plunks herself down in the center of wherever she expects us to be.

Are You not, O God, like Katie? You are aware of our preparations, You predict where we are going, and dash, like the father of the prodigal son, to meet us there. It is not we who arrange ourselves around You. Rather, You place Yourself at our centers. "The kingdom of God is in the midst of you" (Luke 17:21, RSV).

Katie's bedtime romps have taught me that my image of centering on God is a kind of justification by works. I had assumed that I was responsible for organizing my life around God. If I wanted to lead a God-centered life, it was my job to do the centering. I had to go where the Holy One was and wrap myself, as it were, around Her/Him. The initiative and responsibility and the activity was mine. God was passively in place, waiting.

If, however, God is like Katie, then my justification is through grace by faith. The Eternal has entered my life and is rushing to be at its center. That's grace. All I need to do is to believe it, to perceive the Holy One in the middle of the mattress, the middle of the kitchen table, in the rush-hour traffic, the daily paper, the TV screen, the computer console, my mental insights and menial tasks. That's faith.

I don't bring my bed to Katie. She goes before me. If I expect that and look for her there, I easily find her, sitting in the middle of the mattress.

I don't bring my life to God. God goes before me to where my life is going to be. If I expect that and look for the Eternal there, I'll easily find It at the center of my life.

Thirteen

DELIGHT AND DISTURBANCE AT THE CENTER

$\mathscr{S}$ometimes we allow Katie to stay at the center. She sleeps with us. Usually it's very pleasant. She's warm and furry and purry. She snuggles down between us and we chuckle and feel well loved.

God of Love, You are that to me. A source of warmth and enjoyment. You are an experience of being loved.

Sometimes, however, Katie is a darned nuisance. She wakes me up too early, licking my chin with her rasping tongue. She decides it's playtime at three A.M. and leaps from one mound of covers to another.

Thus she interrupts my sleep. But she does

so in such a gentle and enthusiastic and passionate way that I can hardly hold it against her.

O God, are You not like that too? If I let You
stay with me at my center, much of the time it is
grand—warm and loving.

But not always. Sometimes You too are a nuisance. You have purposes. A will to accomplish.
Playfulness to express. You therefore wake me
earlier than I want. You urge me to get started
sooner than is comfortable. You want to work, to
play, to create and have fun, but I want to sleep
because I have to be rested for the coming day.
You act as if Your desires are more important
than my objectives.

When I allow You in my center You both
enhance and disrupt my life. But You do it in
such a mysterious way that I can hardly hold it
against You.

Now that I think about it, I doubt that I

have any choice in deciding whether You will be at the center of my life. I suspect You choose to be there whether I want it that way or not. You are there enhancing and disrupting my life regardless of my wishes.

My only choice is to believe or disbelieve that fact.

Fourteen

. . . .

EXPLORING
CUPBOARDS

*O*ften, while we sit eating, Katie decides to explore the kitchen cupboards. She sniffs. She paws at the cupboard doors. If they are not securely latched, she prys them open and cautiously climbs inside.

She is interested in their dark corners—the concealed clutter, the wastebasket, and the garbage disposal. For some reason she likes to crawl around in the hidden areas of our kitchen.

Holy One, are You like that? Interested in exploring the dark and hidden areas of my life? Does Your love of me include love of the wastebaskets and garbage disposals of my life, the places and processes in which and by which I try to hide and get rid of all my junk, spoilage, and trash?

Katie pokes her nose into our cupboards because she is curious. She is interested but not critical. She does indeed stick her nose into places we do not want her to go, into our hidden housekeeping, but not because she wants either to condemn or improve it. No, she explores these dark cupboards because they intrigue her. She simply wants to know everything about us and our place.

(I do suspect, however, that she hopes she might find something good to eat. This may be her hidden agenda.)

God, is Your love like that? Do You poke around in my dark places, explore my valley of the shadow, simply because I intrigue You? You are interested in all of me. Not only the clean and shiny surfaces but also the dark and smelly interiors where the refuse of my life is hidden. You love it all and none of it repels You. You avoid no part of me.

"Oh God, who hatest nothing that thou hast made . . ." prayed St. Augustine—including my life's wastebaskets and garbage disposals.

And just as Katie explores the sink cabinet because she enjoys doing so, so You explore my hidden life-spaces because You enjoy me. You investigate my darkness, not to find something to condemn but simply to know it. You sniff at the clutter of my concealments, not to find something to get rid of, but simply to know me better.

Therefore I need not fear Your curiosity. I can enjoy Your examination of my life just as I enjoy Katie's examination of our cupboards.

(And maybe, like Katie, You too have a hidden agenda. Maybe You expect to find,

somewhere beneath the shiny countertops,

somewhere behind the closed cupboard
  doors,
something to eat,
something valuable—
something that will please Your desire
and nourish Your purposes.
Something that will add to Your kingdom.)

Fifteen

CLEANSING

$\mathcal{O}$ften when Katie sits beside us she licks her fur. She licks her chest and she licks her legs. She moistens her paw and rubs it over her ears. She licks her tail and chews between her toe pads. She spends a lot of time keeping her fur coat clean.

She also sheds. She leaves cat hair on our sofas, on our chairs, and on our laps. Dead and dirty hairs fall out, to be replaced by live, clean ones.

Thus by licking and shedding she keeps herself clean.

Before Katie came to live with us, I rather assumed that spiritual uncleanness came from within. Indeed, Jesus said something along those lines. "But what comes out of the mouth proceeds from the heart, and this is what defiles. For out of the heart come evil intentions, murder, adultery, fornication, theft, false witness, slander. These are what defile a person, but to eat with unwashed hands does not defile" (Matthew 15:18–20, NRSV).

Katie's cleansing operation suggests another perspective.

As she proceeds through her life she picks up dust and dirt. She cleans it off. She cleans it off in order to keep her fur coat soft, warm, and healthy.

As I go through my life I also accumulate a kind of spiritual dust and dirt. Slight dishonesties and small cruelties are done to me. Specks of neglect, motes of unkindness, bits of injustice, come my way and stick to my soul. I am not only a sinner. I am also sinned against, probably often.

Katie's cat-wash suggests that I also need to spend some time and effort cleaning my soul-fur. Otherwise the sins against me will congeal into a coating of resentment and harden into an armor of defensiveness. They will infect my moral outlook, inviting me to retaliate, corrupting faith into suspicion, hope into cynicism, love into possessiveness.

Not only need I clean up; probably I also need to shed. No doubt there are some soiled soul-fibers that I cannot get clean: worn-out masks that I use to keep the world at a safe distance; habitual deceptions that keep me safe. These psychic patterns may be so deeply stained that they cannot be cleansed, only discarded. This soul-crud, which cannot be restored to clean softness, is better shed.

Life does in fact inflict cruelties and neglects. In truth, life spatters me with spiritual dust, dirt, grease, and scum. And if I let this crud stay on me, I may well become host to spiritual diseases, fleas, and parasites. I will certainly be less attractive to pet. Instead of being soft and warm and inviting, my soul-surface will become greasy, matted, and repellent, sick-looking and sick-feeling.

Katie models for me the daily need to cleanse and shed.

Sixteen

PURRING

AND LOVING

Purring reminds me of loving.

Whenever Katie purrs we assume she is happy. Her body language oozes contentment.

She continually seeks out situations that will start her purring. She'll stretch her neck to receive some scratching behind the ears. She'll arch her back to invite spinal strokes. She'll lie on our laps, stretched full length along our thighs, soaking up our bodily warmth.

She seldom if ever purrs, however, while she is eating. Or when she is playing. She purrs instead when she is close to us, when we are paying attention to her, when our attention is making her feel safe and comfortable.

Katie's purring is a metaphor for human loving. It is her response to our enjoying her, our valuing her, our stroking her, our making her safe and comfortable.

Human loving, Holy One, seems likewise to be our response to Your enjoying us, Your valuing us, Your stroking us, Your making us safe and comfortable.

Loving among us two-legged creatures seems to be our response to the beloved's enjoyment of us. When someone values me highly and consistently, thinks I'm wonderful and wonderful to have around, I label it "being loved." When someone strokes me, my body or my ego, and my psyche glows and my skin tingles, I feel "loved." When I am with someone who makes me feel safe and comfortable, again either physically or psychically, I feel "loved." I tend to respond to attention with loving—just as Katie responds to attention with purring.

But it is more complex for me than it is for cats. Katie purrs. I do not know how to purr. I give back instead more complex responses and I label them "loving." Sometimes, however, the recipient of those responses puts a different label on them—"unloving" submission, exploitation, criticism. Human responses are often not as clear as a cat's purring.

Perhaps the most important truth about loving that Katie's purring teaches me is this: Do not expect the responses to be the same as the strokes. We stroke Katie in one way; scratching behind her ears. She responds in another way; rhythmic rumblings in her throat. We do not get back the same thing we offer.

It's often different with people. I tend to expect, and to want, to receive love in the same style in which I offer it. If I offer admiration, I hope for admiration in return; a simple smile of pleasure seems to be not quite enough. If I offer a hug, I hope to be hugged in return; a handshake feels a bit rejecting. If I offer a kiss, I hope to be kissed back; a plate of brownies is nice but not quite adequate. If I offer money, I hope that at some point money will be returned; a thank-you note does not suffice.

In short, I expect to be loved in the same way I love. I want my beloved's style of loving to be much the same as my own. I want to receive strokes similar to the strokes I give. As someone has said, "We love ourselves the way we have been loved. We love others the way we wish we had been loved." That which I offer is that which I would like returned.

Katie models a different way. She accepts my ways of showing affection. She responds in her way of showing affection. "You love me human-style, I'll love you cat-style. You scratch; I'll purr." That has been a good way of loving for us.

I suspect, O God, that I love You human-style, not cat-style. I expect You to love me the same way I love You. I pay attention to You; I expect You to pay attention to me. I provide You with some money now; I expect You to provide me with financial security later. I value You; I hope You value me. In many ways I love You in the way I want You to love me.

How much better our relationship might be if I acknowledged the fact that we are two different species. You are divine, I am human. Therefore my style of loving You will naturally be different from Your style of loving me.

I stroke and You purr. Grant that,
> when I hear the foundation-shaking rumble
> of Your purr,
> I may recognize it
> as the expression of Your love for me.

or

You stroke and I purr. Grant that
my responsiveness may be
as heartfelt,
as frequent,
and as spontaneous,
as Katie's purring.

Seventeen

UNINTENTIONAL LOVE

Katie's purring is not intentional. It is not a service she performs for my benefit, something done purposefully to please me. No, it is rather part of her spontaneous "cat-ness." When she purrs she is just being her contented cat-self.

So also for human loving. When I "love" in response to others' affection, I am not offering my response as a payment for their attentions. I am not paying them back for what they have given me. I am not intentionally trying to please them. Rather my loving is simply part of my spontaneous human-ness. When I am loving I am just being my contented human-self.

I believe, Holy One, You are to me as I am

to Katie. I offer affection and attention, caresses and warmth, to her. So also You offer affection and attention, strokes and warmth, to me.

And I believe, God, that I am to You as Katie is to me. In my best moments, when I feel touched with Your affection and attention, I "purr," I overflow with spontaneous expressions of delight and contentment. I respond to You as Katie responds to me.

But my responses are often not as whole-hearted as hers. Often they are partial, contrived, intentional: formal worship; contrived niceness; suspicious fear; moral rigidity; cynical scepticism; even outright neglect and rejection. I am not as simple-hearted as Katie.

One reason that I am less responsive than she is that I do not seek out Your presence as Katie seeks out mine. I do not pursue Your attention as Katie pursues mine.

So often she is a presence to me. When I am writing at the word processor she jumps on my lap and tries to stretch out and lie down. She leaps on my desk and parades up and down across my keyboard, rubbing her ears against my chin, begging for a chin-scratch. When I slouch on the couch, reading the newspaper, she climbs on my chest, sticking her nose in my face, sniffing for a caress. When I wash dishes she watches. When I brush my teeth, she paws at my hand. When I take a shower she climbs in between the inner and outer shower curtains and bats at the streaming water. And during meals she sneaks under the table and then leaps up on my lap, making me spill and cuss. She constantly seeks my presence and I continually reward her search with strokes and words. To which she in turn responds by purring.

It is so natural. Both she and I are merely

being who we are. We thoroughly enjoy each
other's company.

Would that I could be thus with You, O God.

Merely being who I am,

constantly seeking Your presence,

thoroughly enjoying Your company,

purring

loving

in contentment.

Eighteen

· · · · · · · · · · ·

DEATH

$\mathcal{K}$atie was killed tonight.

After supper she sat at our apartment door, looking up at us, patiently waiting for her evening walkabout. We let her out, then lowered the cat ladder (a rolled-up carpet) so she could climb up to our balcony when she decided to come home.

She stayed out later than we expected.

My wife went downstairs to see if, by some chance, she was waiting at the door. She came back stiff-faced. "There's a cat lying in the middle of the street."

I went downstairs. I saw the body. "It's not Katie," I said to myself. "There's too much white."

But it was Katie.

She was still warm when I picked her up. She lolled in my arms just as she had when she was alive—paws sticking out, head in the crook of my elbow. I carried her to the door. My wife was waiting.

We cried.

We loved that cat.

I carried her upstairs to our apartment, half-numb, half-hoping it wasn't true, cradling her as if she were still alive.

God damn it to hell, god damn it to hell!

Katie had an old towel on which she liked to sit. We wrapped her in it. We laid her on the living room floor and cried.

We did not know what to do next.

Finally we carried her body to our garage. We found there an old beer carton. It was, in its own way, a friendly and familiar box—one that had been with us through several of our moves. We put Katie in it, wrapped in her towel. It felt cheap and inadequate but we didn't know what else to do.

We went back upstairs and cried some more and remembered.

Gradually I became aware that I wanted to bring her body to St. Joseph's, my church, to its chapel. More and more it seemed right to do so. Even if she was a cat, she was a loved and loving cat, and that which is loved and loving belongs to God and is of God. So we took her body to the chapel and prayed and wept and remembered.

I know of no reason to believe that cats are not souls. It seemed at that moment that human arrogance was the only explanation for the claim that only human beings are souls. O God, if You are the God of the loving, You are the God of Katie as much as You are my God. If You are the source of all being, You are her source as well as mine. It seems right to have honored her and honored You by bringing her body, in its cardboard beer carton and faded towel, to Your altar, that You might have mercy on us all.

Even as I write this, O God, it suddenly seems unreal. This cannot have happened. It is too evil.

I loved her.

I have never been very confident of my ability to love. It has often seemed so difficult to feel affection for many of the people for whom I am supposed to feel affection.

But I know, now, that I am able to love—more able than I thought—because I know I loved Katie.

This knowledge, this experience, is Katie's last gift to me.

> My cat has been my shepherd. I no longer want.

She has laid down with me on brown sofas.
She has led me through quiet thoughtfulness;
   she has restored my soul.
She has led me in paths of playfulness for
   that was her nature.
Even though we now walk in the valley of
   the shadow of death,
I do not fear that evil will destroy love.

Nineteen

AFTERMATH

This morning I washed Katie's dish for the last time. Had she not been killed, she would have been watching me, perched on an end table in the hall, peering in the kitchen door. Running water fascinated her.

We gathered up her things. I took them to the garage. She had only a small estate. A cat box. A traveling cage. A leash. A scratching post. Leftover cat food and cat litter. A ball of green yarn, a ball with a bell on it, a cloth mouse, a string with a piece of newspaper tied at the end of it. Not much.

"Blessed are the poor, for theirs is the kingdom of heaven."

She never tried to accumulate things. She trusted us to provide whatever she needed, even more than she could imagine. (We provided everything but safety.) This, of course, is not surprising. She was, after all, a cat.

Do You, O God, intend that all Your creatures live in this way? Is it Your plan that all of us live simply, trusting You to provide what we need, even more than we can imagine? Do You intend that we end our lives with only small estates?

And do You, too, provide everything, O God, except safety?

We allowed Katie to live her life, to go out when she wanted to, even though we knew there were substantial risks from the traffic in the street fronting our apartment. There were large lawns in back of the apartment complex and we hoped that Katie would choose the grassland rather than the roadway. Or that, if she chose the road, she would be smart enough and quick enough to protect herself.

It didn't work out the way we hoped.

Is it that way for You too, Lord? You are aware of the dangers, yet You allow us to live our lives, hoping we will choose safe lawns to play in. Or at least, if we choose to explore dangerous roads, You hope we will be quick and careful in order that we might live.

And if we die too soon, run down by the technology of our time, do You not grieve—cry and curse—for us as we do now for our little cat? If we so love and enjoy that friendly ball of fur, how much more do You love and enjoy us?

Perhaps we were so easily able to love her because she was so poor. She had so little and was content to have only that. Perhaps if we also had little, and were similarly content, we too would be easier to love.

Twenty

. . . .

ONE
LAST TRIP

Fifty yards east of St. Joseph's Parish Center there is a ravine, a little drainage streambed.

We buried Katie on its banks this afternoon. I borrowed a shovel from the church tool room. My wife held the box containing Katie's body as we drove to the place. She said, "One last trip, Katie."

I remembered our other trips, to the veternarian, to our summer place. Katie would move around the car—up on the dashboard, down under the seat, up on the rear window ledge, down under the brake pedal, curl on our laps, climb on our shoulders. At the beginning of any trip she was constantly on the move.

On this trip of course she was still.

We went to worship this morning. When we returned we found an envelope under our apartment door. Inside was a prayer, a memorial for Katie. It was unsigned. It think it was from someone from St. Joe's. We read it and cried. We prayed it as we buried Katie.

And so it ends, the insistent, funny, affectionate, evocative company of our cat. The love does not end, I think. We care and will continue to care. We remember and will continue to remember and the recollections will both pain and please us.

One last trip.

Katie, are you now one of that "cloud of witnesses" (Hebrews 12:1) who surround and cheer on the faithful? God, in Your mercy, do You designate a place in heaven's bleachers for pet cats? Special memberships in the communion of saints for four-legged lovers?